BRINGING DOWN THE LIGHT

JOURNEY OF A SOUL AFTER DEATH

PAINTINGS by MOTHER MEERA

MEERAMMA PUBLICATIONS,   ITHACA, NEW YORK

Meeramma Publications
26 Spruce Lane
Ithaca, New York 14850
USA
(607) 257 1715

Printed in Hong Kong

ISBN: 0-9622973-2-1

Library of Congress Cataloging-in-Publication Data

Meera, Mother, 1960–
    Bringing down the light : journey of a soul after death / Mother
Meera.
    64p.   cm.
    ISBN 0–9622973–2–1 : $29.95
    1. Spirit art.   I. Title.
BF1313.M44 1989
    133.9'3—dc20   89–13577
                                                         CIP

"We have to try to reveal that Light which is in us as a bud. It must blossom like a flower. In all things everywhere, in all beings the light is hidden, and it must be revealed. If we try with all our hearts we will be successful . . . . We will live perpetually in the Paramatman Light and be Paramatman. I want the Paratmatman Light to blossom everywhere."

INTRODUCTION

This exquisite and sacred series of twenty-four paintings by one of the greatest Masters of our age, Mother Meera, is an unique artistic and spiritual document. It represents Mother's direct visionary insight into the worlds after death and the journey of a close disciple and great soul after he left his body.

There have been many spiritual artists who have recorded their visions (we think of Blake, of the finest Tibetan tangka painters, of certain anonymous Egyptian masters, of Samuel Palmer and Signorelli); but no-one of comparable spiritual stature to the Mother, who is worshipped by her devotees as an incarnation of the Divine Mother herself, has ever before graced mankind with so simple, poignant, and tender a glimpse into the inner worlds. Mother has said that the painting of these works gave her great joy and that they show exactly what she knew and saw—the states through which the soul travels after death. They represent, then, a silent immediate transmission of the highest knowledge, a gift by the Divine Mother to her children of hope and visionary assurance.

Death frightens nearly every human being, even those who have achieved real spiritual insight; these paintings of the radiant worlds and spheres of the soul's journey after death, of the beauty of the Forces that accompany the soul, of the splendor, soft and infinitely supple, of the immeasurably more gentle universe that exists beyond the confines of the flesh, cannot fail to bring some power of strong hope to all of us.

The after-death experience portrayed in these paintings refers very particularly to Mother Meera's protector and devotee Mr. Reddy. His journey, because of his state of development and devotion to the Divine was an unique one. Mr. Reddy was born in India in 1925 and lived a life of the deepest and bravest dedication to God. All his youth he searched for the Divine Mother, longing to encounter her in a body here on the earth. After a long, often painful and exhausting inner journey, Mr. Reddy did eventually find the Divine Mother—in Meera, his own relative, who was then a very young girl. Slowly, dazzlingly, the girl revealed to him her Divine Identity and Mr. Reddy became her devotee, "father," protector, spiritual companion, and herald. After a long illness he died in Germany in 1985.

Mother has said that Mr. Reddy came to the world with the special mission of discovering, protecting and announcing her to mankind, and that he was, in Indian terms, a vibhuti, a soul with a special divine mission. She has also said that through the intensity of his devotion to her and her work of world transformation through bringing down the Divine Paramatman Light into the lower levels of creation, Mr. Reddy's soul, already magnificently rich and expansive, achieved an even greater status and earned, as we see in these paintings, the particular cosmic protectiveness and rapturous consoling guidance after death of many aspects of the Mother—Durga, Sweet Mother, and others that are not named.

Although no-one can have the relationship with Mother Meera that Mr. Reddy enjoyed, she has said that all those who truly love her and look to her love for help will be guided by her in all the worlds after death. There can be no abandonment of the loving soul by the Mother; the soul that has turned to God in any form is helped in its long evolution towards complete Union with the Divine, helped with something of the unfathomable joy and beauty and grace that these paintings show.

Every man or woman who contemplates these works can feel something of his or her own journey mirrored in them. From her grief at Mr. Reddy's death and her compassion for all her children who face death, the Mother made these works to inspire all men and women to love God with something of Mr. Reddy's passion, to give mankind a glimpse of the cosmic rapture that such devoted passion evokes in the heart of the Divine. A sublime mystery of reciprocated love between the soul and God, the child and the Mother, suffuses with its light these astonishing paintings. To know and live and enact that mystery consciously is the prayer and the work of every lover of God in the body as well as beyond it.

What is the nature of those who journey through the shifting and luminous landscapes depicted in these paintings? Mother Meera has said that it is the soul's body of light that continues after death. Although there may be some variation in its form that accords with the development of the individual soul, all human souls inhabit a soft and supple vehicle similar to that of Mr. Reddy.

During our lives the soul acts as a protector, remaining with us through their unfolding sequence until we attain Union with the Divine. Between lives it continues its development within the rich experiences afforded by the subtle realms and through the direct loving guidance of the Mother—she who helps us negotiate in death, as in life, the path to the Divine.

These paintings of the worlds beyond death give hope to all of us, still searching in a body. They tell us, with the incandescent directness of the one who painted them, that the Mother is here; that her Light is everywhere penetrating the creation and enabling it to flower; that the world, faced with unprecedented dangers is also being given unprecedented help to develop and transform its ancient darkness into knowledge and bliss. What more consoling and emboldening message could mankind be given at this moment?

May all those who meet these paintings now in their privacy find the Light that is hidden in them, and the guidance of that Light to the heart of their own secret.

Andrew Harvey
Thalheim
August 18, 1989

VORWORT

Dieser exquisite und geheiligte Zyklus, bestehend aus 24 Aquarellen, von einem der grössten Meister unserer Zeit "Mother Meera", ist ein einzigartiges künstlerisches und spirituelles Zeugnis. Es gibt Mother Meera's unmittelbare visionäre Schau in die Welten nach dem Tod wieder und die Reise eines vertrauten Schülers und einer grossen Seele, nachdem er seinen Körper verlassen hat.

Es hat viele spirituelle Künstler gegeben, die ihre Visionen aufgezeichnet haben. Wir denken an Blake, an herausragende Tibetanische Tangka-Maler, an Samuel Palmer und Signorelli. Nie hat jedoch eine Persönlichkeit von vergleichbarer geistiger Statur wie Mother Meera, die als Inkarnation der Göttlichen Mutter selbst verehrt wird—die Menschheit mit einem so unkomplizierten, treffenden und sanften Aufleuchten der inneren Welten begnadet.

Mother Meera sagt, dass ihr das Malen dieser Werke grosse Freude bereitete und dass sie genau wiedergeben, was sie wusste und sah: die Zustände, die der Seele nach dem Tod widerfahren. Sie ermöglichen eine stille und unmittelbare Weitergabe höchstmöglichen Wissens, ein Geschenk der Göttlichen Mutter an ihre Kinder, Hoffnung und visionäre Zusicherung zugleich.

Der Tod erschreckt nahezu jedes menschliche Wesen, sogar jene, denen sich wahrhafte spirituelle Einsichten eröffnet haben. Diese Biler strahlender Welten und Sphären, die seelisch nach dem Tod beschritten werden, die Schönheit der sie begleitenden Mächte, der Glanz, sanft und unendlich schmiegsam, das unermesslich subtile Universum, das unabhängig von den Begrenzungen des Körperlich-Materiellen besteht— sie können nicht anders als die wunderbare Kraft einer starken Hoffnung in uns allen erwecken.

Die Nach-dem-Tod-Erfahrung, die durch diese Aquarelle verständlich wird, bezieht sich ganz besonders auf Mother Meera's Förderer und Devotee Mr. Reddy. Die Reise dieser Seele war aufgrund seiner Reife und aussergewöhnlichen Hingabe an das Göttliche einzigartig. Mr. Reddy, der

1925 in Indien geboren wurde, führte ein Leben entschiedenster und tiefster Gottergebenheit. Seine Jugend war einzig der Suche der Göttlichen Mutter gewidmet in dem sehnsüchtigen Verlagen, ihrer Inkarnation auf der Erde zu begegnen. Nach einem langen, oft mühseligen und erschöpfenden inneren Werdegang fand Mr. Reddy schliesslich die Göttliche Mutter in Meera, damals einem noch jungen Mädchen, das sogar mit ihm verwandt war. Überwältigend enthüllte ihm das Mädchen nach und nach seine göttliche Herkunft und Mr. Reddy wurde ihr Devotee, Vater, Förderer, spiritueller Weggefährte und Verkünder. Nach langer Krankheit starb Mr. Reddy 1985 in Deutschland.

Mother Meera sagt, dass Mr. Reddy's Leben dazu auserkoren war, sie zu entdecken, zu fördern und der Menschheit kundzutun und dass er nach indischen Begriffen ein "vibhuti" war, eine Seele mit besonderer göttlicher Aufgabe. Ferner sagt Mother Meera, dass Mr. Reddy's wunderbar reiche Seele durch die bedingungslose, intensive Hingabe an sie selbst und für ihre Arbeit, der Transformation der Welt durch das Herabbringen des göttlichen Paramatman-Lichtes, einen noch höheren Adel erwarb und verdiente, und des besonderen kosmischen Schutzes und der tröstenden und beglückenden Führung nach dem Tod durch viele Ausdrucksformen der Mutter—Durga, Sweet Mother und andere, die nicht genannt sind, würdig wurde, so wie wir es in diesen Bildern erkennen können.

Obwohl niemand die Beziehung zu Mother Meera haben kann, der sich Mr. Reddy erfreute, lässt Mother Meera wissen, dass alle, die sie wahrhaft lieben und sich hilfesuchend ihrer Liebe anvertrauen, nach dem Tode in allen Welten führen wird. Eine liebende Seele wird nie von der Mutter preisgegeben. Eine Seele, die sich Gott—in welcher Weise auch immer— zuwandte, ist der Hilfe auf ihrer langen Evolution bis zur völligen Vereinigung mit dem Göttlichen gewiss, ihr wird von der unergründlichen Freude, Schönheit und Anmut, die diese Bilder erkennen lassen, zuteil.

Der unvoreingenommene Betrachter dieser Werke wird in ihnen etwas von seinem eigenen Lebensgang reflektiert sehen. Die Trauer über Mr. Reddy's Heimgang und ihr Mitgefühl mit all ihren Kindern angesichts des Todes, bewegte Mother Meera diese Gemälde zu schaffen um in allen Menschen die Begeisterung zu wecken, Gott zu lieben, wenn auch nicht in dem Ausmass, so doch mit der Qualität der Leidenschaft wie Mr. Reddy sie lebte; ebenso möchte sie die Menschheit mit einem Schimmer des kosmischen Entzückens beglücken, die eine derartige hingebungsvolle Leidenschaft im göttlichen Herzen erwecken kann.

Ein hehres Mysterium erwiderter Liebe zwischen Seele und Gott, dem Kind und der Mutter, durchflutet mit seinem Licht diese in Verwunderung versetzende Bilder. Dieses Mysterium zu erkennen, zu leben und in die Tat umzusetzen, bewusst, ist Anrufung und Werk eines jeden Gottliebenden sowohl in siener Körperlichkeit als auch über sie hinaus.

Welche Wesen sind es, die diese wechselnden, helleuchtenden Sphären betreten, die diese Gemälde zeigen? Mother Meera sagt, dass es der Lichtkörper der Seele ist, der nach dem Tod fortbesteht. Obwohl sich gewisse Unterschiede in seiner Gestalt ausdrücken, die mit der Entwicklung der individuellen Seele übereinstimmen, bewohnen doch alle menschlichen Seelen so sanfte und geschmeidige Hüllen, ähnlich der von Mr. Reddy.

Zeit unseres Lebens agiert die Seele als Beschützerin und verweilt durch alle Entwicklungsstufen hindurch bei uns bis wir eins mit den Göttlichen sind. Von Leben zu Leben setzt sie ihre Entwicklung im Bereich der reichen Erfahrungsmöglichkeiten fort, welche die subtilen Existenzebenen gewähren unter der unmittelbaren, liebevollen Führung der Mutter, die uns hilft, den Tod zu überwinden und im Leben zu bestehen, auf dem Pfad zum Göttlichen.

Diese Bilder, die von den Welten zeugen, die über die Grenzen des Todes hinausgehen, geben uns allen, die wir suchen, gebunden durch den Körper, Hoffnung. Sie teilen uns mit, mit der glühenden Herzlichkeit derjenigen, die sie malte, dass die Mutter hier ist; dass ihr Licht allgegenwärtig ist, die Schöpfung durchdringt und ihr ermöglicht zu blühen; dass die Welt angesichts noch nie dagewesener Gefahren, eine machtvolle beispiellose Hilfe gewährt wird, damit sie sich entfalten und ihre uralte Dunkelheit in Wissen und Glückseligkeit verwandeln kann.

Gibt es in diesem Augenblick eine Botschaft, die die Menschheit mehr zu ermutigen und zu trösten vermag?

Mögen alle, denen diese Gemälde im Vertrauen überlassen sind, das Licht, das in ihnen verborgen ist, finden und von diesem Licht zum Herzen ihres eigenen Seins geleitet sein.

Andrew Harvey
Thalheim
den 18. August 1989

INTRODUCTION

Cette merveilleuse série de 24 tableaux sacrés, peints par Mère Meera, l'un des plus grands Maîtres de notre temps, est un document spirituel et artistique unique. Mère Meera nous ouvre sa vision directe et pénétrante sur les mondes après la mort, ainsi que le voyage d'un proche disciple, d'une grande âme, après qu'il ait quitté son corps.

De nombreux artistes spirituels nous ont retransmis leurs visions (nous pensons à Blake par exemple, ou bien encore aux peintres des plus belles tangka tibétaines, à certains maîtres Egyptiens anonymes, à Samuel Palmer et à Signorelli). Aucun cependant, d'une stature spirituelle comparable à celle de Mère,—vénérée par ses disciples comme l'incarnation de la Mère Divine—n'a jamais su transmettre à l'humanité ces mondes intérieurs avec une expression si simple, si tendre et si forte. Mère Meera dit que la peinture de ces tableaux lui a procuré une grande joie et qu'ils illustrent exactement ce qu'elle a vu et ce qu'elle sait sur les états que traverse l'âme après la mort. Ces tableaux sont donc la transmission du plus haut savoir, un don d'espoir et de promesse visionnaire de la Mère Divine à ses enfants.

La mort effraie presque tous les êtres humains, même ceux qui ont atteint une réalisation spirituelle certaine. Ces illustrations sont de sphères et de mondes radieux que traverse l'âme après la mort, la beauté des puissances les accompagnant, la splendeur éclatante quoique douce et infiniment attendrissante d'un univers subtil qui existe au-delà des limitations de nos corps matérialisés. Ils ne peuvent qu'éveiller en nous une prodigieuse force et un espoir sans limite.

L'expérience de l'après-mort, illustrée sur ces tableaux, fait directement allusion au protecteur et disciple M. Reddy. Le voyage de cette âme porte un caractère exceptionnel, tout en union avec son développement spirituel et sa dévotion au Divin. M. Reddy est né aux Indes en 1925 et a mené une vie courageuse et entièrement dédiée à Dieu. Sa jeunesse était toute imbue du désir de rencontrer la Mère Divine incarnée ici sur terre. Après un long chemin intérieur souvent douloureux et épuisant, M. Reddy finit par découvrir la Mère Divine, en Meera, une parente qui était alors une toute petite fille. Peu à peu, l'éblouissant de son éclat, la fillette lui révéla son identité divine et M. Reddy lui consacra sa vie, "père", protecteur, compagnon spirituel, héraut. Il mourut en 1985, en Allemagne, après une longue maladie.

Mère a dit que M. Reddy est venu au monde avec la mission spéciale de la découvrir, de la protéger et de l'annoncer à l'humanité. Il était, en terme indien, un vibhuti, une âme dotée d'une mission divine particulière. Mère Meera dit encore qu'en raison de la merveilleuse richesse de son âme, de sa dévotion complète à son égard et envers la mission qu'elle remplit sur terre—la transformation du monde par la descente de la lumière divine sur toute la création—, M. Reddy acquit une noblesse d'âme encore plus grande. Cela lui a valu après sa mort, comme nous le voyons dans ces tableaux, la protection cosmique et l'aide consolante et enivrante de la Mère Divine sous ses différents aspects: Durga, Douce Mère et d'autres non nommés.

Bien que personne ne puisse jouir du même rapport que celui qui existait entre Mère Meera et M. Reddy, Mère nous fait savoir que tous ceux qui l'aiment vraiment et se tournent vers son amour quand ils ont besoin d'aide, seront guidés par elle dans tous les mondes après la mort. Aucune âme aimante ne peut être abandonnée par la Mère; une âme qui s'est tournée vers Dieu, de quelque façon que se soit, sera assistée dans sa longue évolution, jusqu'à l'Union complète avec le Divin. Elle sera soutenue par l'inépuisable bonheur, la beauté et la grâce qui émanent de ces tableaux.

Tout homme ou femme, qui contemple ces oeuvres, retrouve en elles comme le reflet de son propre voyage. Puissante dans sa douleur à la mort de M. Reddy et dans sa compassion pour tous ses enfants face à la mort, Mère a peint ces oeuvres pour nous inciter à aimer Dieu passionnément, comme nous l'a témoigné M. Reddy et elle nous montre l'extase cosmique qu'une telle passion fait naître dans le coeur du Divin. Ces tableaux étonnants reflètent les rayons lumineux du mystère sublime de l'amour entre l'âme et Dieu, entre l'enfant et la Mère Divine. S'abandonner au mystère de l'amour, se laisser enrichir par sa lumière, telle est la fervente prière et la volonté de chaque amant de Dieu ici-bas, autant que dans l'au-delà.

Quelle est la nature de ceux qui traversent les paysages changeants et lumineux dépeints dans ces tableaux? Mère Meera a dit qu'il s'agit du corps lumineux de l'âme qui survit à la mort. Bien qu'il y ait certaines variations dans leurs formes, selon le développement de l'âme individuelle, toutes les âmes humaines habitent une enveloppe souple et molle semblable à celle de M. Reddy.

Tout au long de nos vies, l'âme nous protège, restant avec nous jusqu'à ce que nous atteignions l'Union avec le Divin. Sous la conduite aimante et directe de Mère, qui est notre médiatrice sur la voie vers Dieu—dans la mort comme dans la vie—, l'âme continue son développement entre nos vies, à l'intérieur des riches expériences offertes par les mondes subtils.

Ces représentations des mondes de l'au-delà donnent grand espoir à tous ceux qui cherchent alors qu'ils sont encore incarnés. Ils nous dévoilent avec la simplicité et la profondeur lumineuse de celle qui les a peints, que la Mère est ici; que la lumière est partout, pénétrant la création et lui permettant de s'épanouir; que le monde, en ce moment, fait face à des dangers sans précédent, mais reçoit aussi une aide équivalente lui permettant de se développer et de transformer l'ombre de l'ignorance en savoir et extase. Quel message plus consolant et plus encourageant pourait-on donner à l'humanité en ce moment?

Que ceux qui reçoivent ces visions au plus profond de leur être trouvent la Lumière qui y est cachée et que cette Lumière les guide au coeur de leur propre secret.

Andrew Harvey
Thalheim
18 août 1989

BRINGING DOWN
THE LIGHT

June 19, 1985 (one day before Mr. Reddy's death)

It is a stormy day; nature is full of sorrow. In Mr. Reddy's farmyard in India stands a tree under which is a tub filled with water for animals to drink. Mr. Reddy, dressed in typical Indian fashion, sits near the feet of the Mother and looks at her.

19. Juni 1985 (einen Tag vor Herrn Reddy Ableben)

Es ist ein stürmischer Tag, die Natur ist voller Trauer. Unter einem Baum auf Herrn Reddys Bauernhof in Indien steht eine Viehtränke. Herr Reddy, typisch indisch gekleidet, sitzt zu den Füssen der Mutter und schaut sie an.

19 juin 1985 (un jour avant la mort de M. Reddy)

Jour de tempête: la nature est emplie de tristesse. Aux Indes, dans la cour de la ferme de M. Reddy, on voit un arbre, sous lequel se trove un bassin rempli d'eau dans lequel boivent les animaux. M. Reddy, en costume indien, est assis au pied de la Mère et la regarde.

June 21, 1985

Mr. Reddy (white figure) with the Divine Mother (blue figure). Because the painting is depicting a process, the white figure appears on both the left and the right of the painting.

21. Juni 1985

Herr Reddy (weisse Gestalt) und die Göttliche Mutter (blaue Gestalt). Da das Bild einen Vorgang darstellt, erscheint die weisse Gestalt auf der linken wei auf der rechten Seite.

21 juin 1985

M. Reddy (forme blanche) avec la Mère Divine (forme bleue). Puisque le tableau dépeint un processus, la silhouette blanche apparaît, à la fois, à gauche et à droite du tableau.

June 23, 1985
Mr. Reddy's soul (the white figure) merging with the Mother.

23. Juni 1985
Herrn Reddys Seele (die weisse Gestalt) verschmilzt mit der Mutter.

23 juin 1985
L'âme de M. Reddy (la forme blanche) se confond avec la Mère.

MR.REDDY
23.6.1985 M.M

July 19, 1985

Sri Aurobindo tells Sweet Mother, "Our baby (red figure) is coming." The three travel in a boat.

19. Juli 1985

Sri Aurobindo sagt zu Sweet Mother: "Unser Kind (rote Gestalt) kommt." Die drei fahren in einem Boot.

19 juillet 1985

Sri Aurobindo dit à Douce Mère: "Notre bébé (forme rouge) arrive". Ils voyagent tous trois en bateau.

August 3, 1985
Mr. Reddy and the Mother embrace each other.

3. August 1985
Herr Reddy und die Mutter umarmen sich.

3 août 1985
M. Reddy et la Mère s'étreignent.

November 4, 1985
When Mr. Reddy embraces the Divine Mother, his soul joins
Paramatman.

4. November 1985
Als Herr Reddy die Göttliche Mutter umarmt, verbindet sich seine
Seele mit Paramatman.

4 novembre 1985
Quand M. Reddy étreint la Mère Divine, son âme rejoint
Paramatman.

November 6, 1985

Mr. Reddy is happy to hold the Paramatman light.

6. November 1985

Herr Reddy ist glücklich darüber, das Paramatman-Licht in sich zu tragen.

6 novembre 1985

M. Reddy est heureux de tenir la lumière Paramatman.

6-11-1985

M.M

March 20, 1986

Because Mr. Reddy is weak, he is lying down. The Mother is show-
ing the Paramatman light to him. Humbly, he is doing namaskaram
to Paramatman.

20. Marz 1986

Herr Reddy hat sich hingelegt, weil er schwach ist. Die Mutter zeigt
ihm das Paramatman-Licht. Demütig macht er ''namaskaram'' vor
Paramatman.

20 mars 1986

Parce qu'il est faible, M. Reddy est étendu. La Mère lui montre la
lumière Paramatman. Humblement il fait ''namaskaram'' à
Paramatman.

August 20, 1986

Mr. Reddy sits down to meditate, but is disturbed by many thoughts.

20. August 1986

Herr Reddy setzt sich zur Meditation nieder, wird jedoch durch viele Gedanken abgelenkt.

20 août 1986

M. Reddy s'assied pour méditer, mais il est troublé par de nombreuses pensées.

20-8-1986
M.M

August 21, 1986

The many thoughts that have come to Mr. Reddy in meditation have abated; a tree appears.

21. August 1986

Die Gedankenflut in Herrn Reddys Meditation hat sich gelegt; ein Baum erscheint.

21 août 1986

Les pensées qui assaillaient M. Reddy durant sa méditation sont vaincues. Un arbre surgit.

August 22, 1986

After the quietening of Mr. Reddy's meditation and the appearance of a tree, Mr. Reddy sees Mother Durga. She appears in a blue form instead of her usual red one in order to test his discernment, that is, to see whether or not he can feel that the figure he sees is truly her.

22. August 1986

Nachdem Herrn Reddys Meditation ruhig geworden und ein Baum erschienen ist, sieht Herr Reddy die Mutter Durga. Sie zeigt sich in einer blauen Gestalt, statt ihrer üblichen roten, um seine Unterscheidungskraft zu prüfen, d.h. um zu sehen, ob er fühlt, dass die Gestalt, die er wahrnimmt, wirklich sie ist.

22 août 1986

Après que le calme est rétabli et que l'arbre est apparu, M. Reddy voit Mère Durga. Elle se montre sous une forme bleue, au lieu du rouge habituel, pour mettre à l'épreuve la capacité de discernement de M. Reddy, c'est-à-dire, pour voir si oui ou non, il se rend compte que c'est vraiment elle.

August 23, 1986

Because Mr. Reddy, recognizing Mother Durga's presence, thinks that her form should be red, Durga changes from blue to red.

23. August 1986

Da Herr Reddy, der die Gegenwart der Mutter Durga erkennt, denkt, dass ihre Gestalt rot sein müsse, wechselt Durga von blau zu rot.

23 août 1986

Puisque M. Reddy, qui reconnaît la présence de Mère Durga, pense que la forme de celle-ci devrait être rouge, Durga passe du bleu au rouge.

September 24, 1986

One of the Mothers is taking care of Mr.Reddy while the others look on.

24. September 1986

Eine der Mütter sorgt für Herrn Reddy, während die anderen zusehen.

24 septembre 1986

L'une des Mères prend soin de M. Reddy pendant que les autres observent.

24.9.1986

October 10, 1986

Mr. Reddy tells the Mother that he cannot walk any more; she
takes him into her arms.

10. October 1986

Herr Reddy sagt der Mutter, er könne nicht mehr laufen. Sie nimmt
ihn in die Arme.

10 octobre 1986

M. Reddy dit à la Mère qu'il ne peut plus marcher; elle le prend
dans ses bras.

10-10-1986
Amma

December 7, 1986

Mr. Reddy is lying down on the grass with his head in the Mother's lap. A being blesses him, and he travels to the higher worlds, finally joining in Paramatman.

7. Dezember 1986

Herr Reddy streckt sich auf dem Gras aus, seinen Kopf in den Schoss der Mutter gebettet. Ein Wesen segnet ihn, er reist in die höheren Welten und geht schliesslich in Paramatman ein.

7 décembre 1986

M. Reddy est étendu dans l'herbe avec la tête sur les genoux de la Mère. Un être le benit, et il voyage dans les plus hautes sphères, se fondant enfin dans Paramatman.

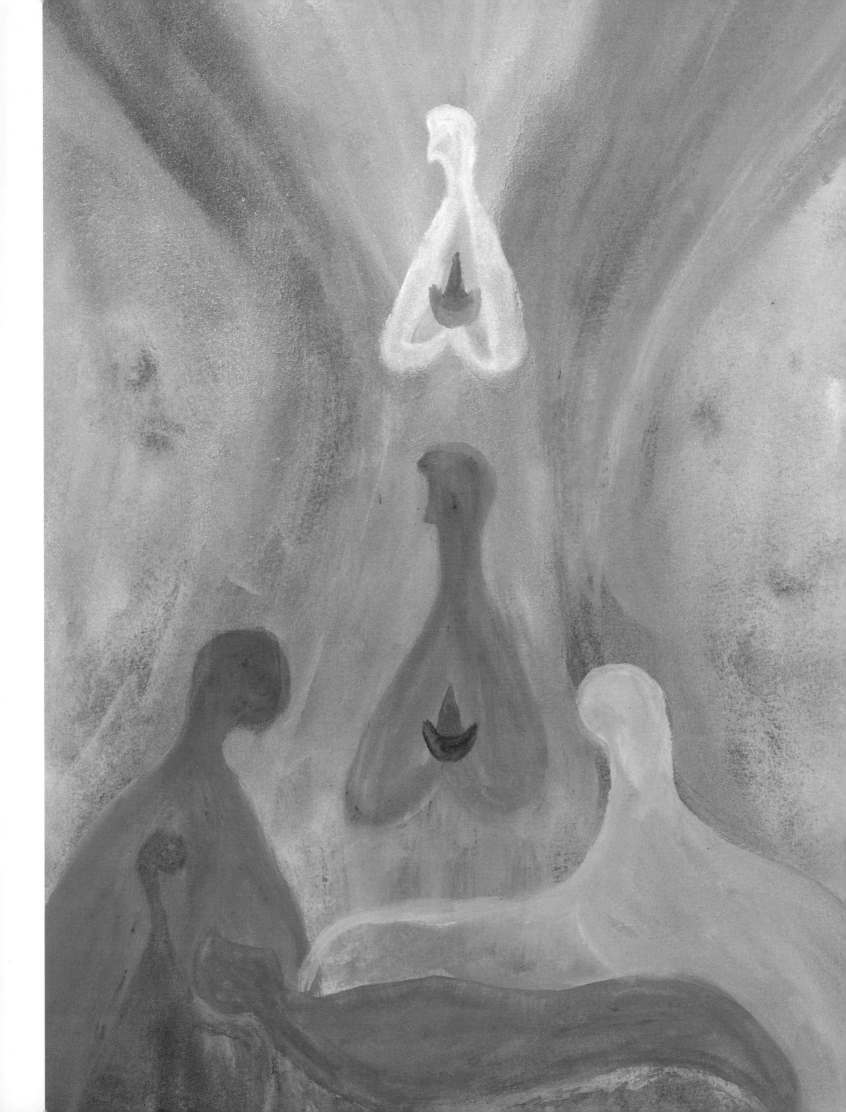

December 11, 1986
The Mother and Mr. Reddy bringing down the light.

11. Dezember 1986
Die Mutter und Herr Reddy beim Herabbringen des Lichts.

11 décembre 1986
La Mère et M. Reddy font descendre la lumière.

December 12, 1986
Mr. Reddy is one with the Mother.

12. Dezember 1986
Herr Reddy ist eins mit der Mutter.

12 décembre 1986
M. Reddy est un avec la Mère.

12-12-86
Amma

January 20, 1987

The Mother holds Mr. Reddy in her arms. Afterwards (on left), Mr. Reddy gradually descends into the Mother.

20. Januar 1987

Die Mutter hält Herrn Reddy in den Armen. Danach (links) sinkt Herr Reddy langsam in die Mutter hinein.

20 janvier 1987

La Mère tient M. Reddy dans ses bras. Plus tard (à gauche) M. Reddy descend graduellement dans la Mère.

February 21, 1987

Lying on the peaks of a mountain that represents majesty, Mr.
Reddy holds the light.

21. Februar 1987

Herr Reddy hält das Licht. Er ruht auf den Gipfeln eines Berges,
der Erhabenheit bedeutet.

21 février 1987

Etendu au sommet d'une montagne, signe de majesté, M. Reddy
tient la lumière.

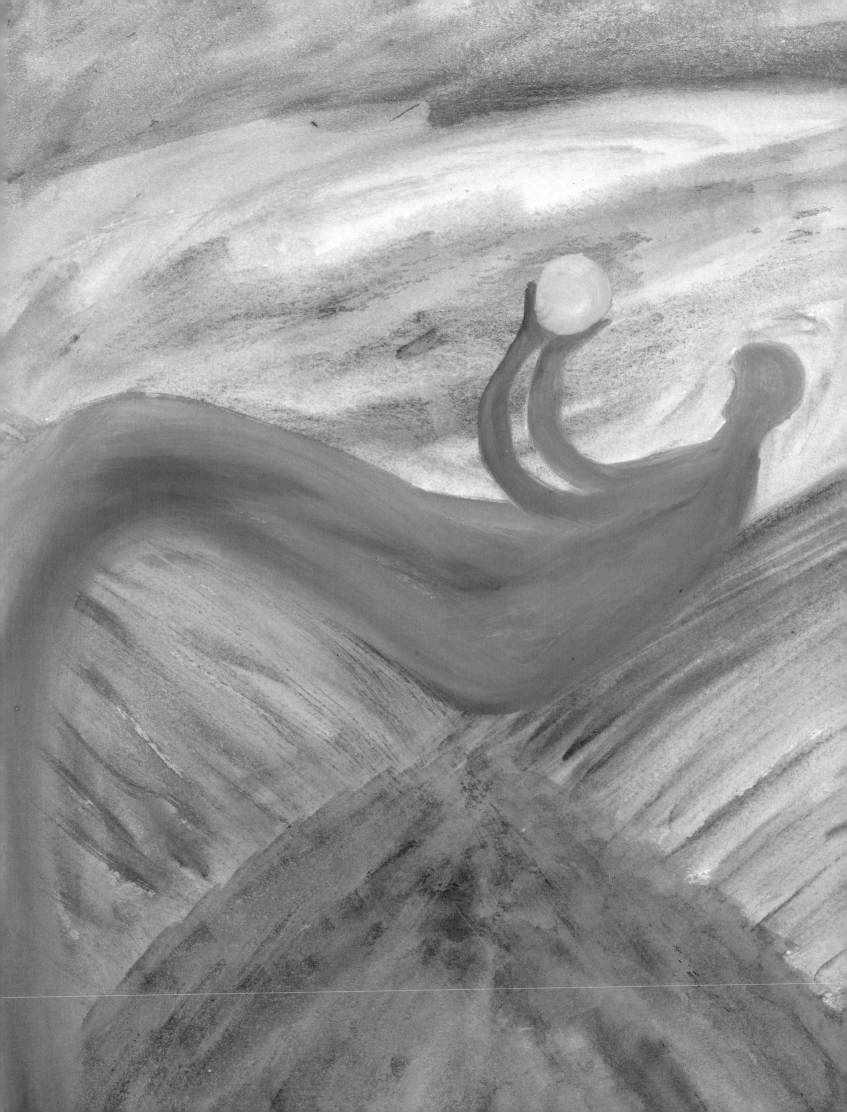

May 22, 1987
Mr. Reddy and the Mother are inside the Peaceful Cave.

22. Mai 1987
Herr Reddy und die Mutter in der ''Friedvollen Grotte''.

22 mai 1987
M. Reddy et la Mère sont à l'intérieur de la Cave Paisible.

22.5.1987
M.M

August 3, 1987
Mr. Reddy offers flowers to the Mother.

3. August 1987
Herr Reddy bringt der Mutter Blumen dar.

3 août 1987
M. Reddy offre des fleurs à la Mère.

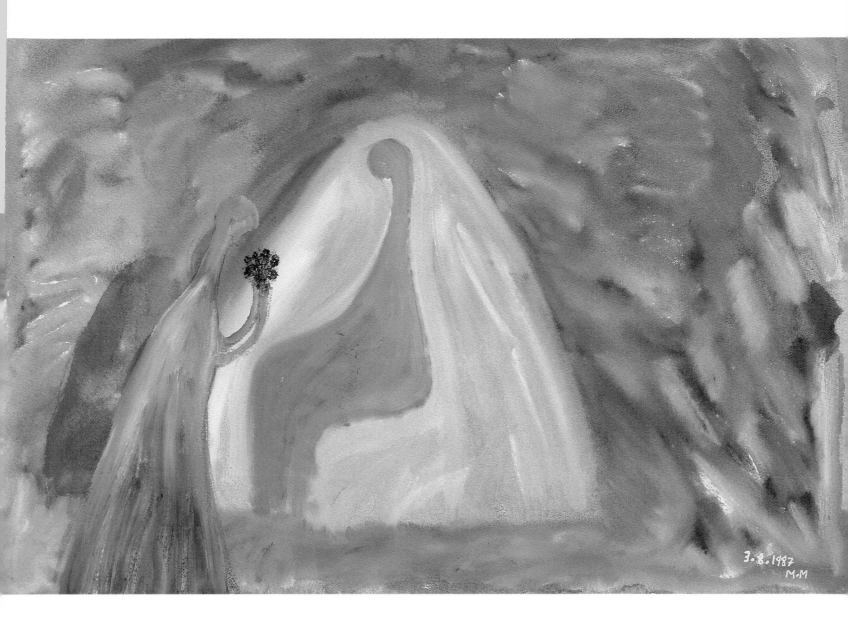

August 8, 1987
Mr. Reddy's subtle glimpse.

8. August 1987
Herrn Reddys subtiler Einblick.

8 août 1987
La vision subtile de M. Reddy.

8.8.1987
M.M

November 8, 1987

Two Mothers are sitting inside the Peaceful Cave with Mr. Reddy between them.

8. November 1987

Zwei Mütter sitzen in der "Friedvollen Grotte", zwischen ihnen Herr Reddy.

8 novembre 1987

Deux Mères sont assises à l'intérieur de la Cave Paisible. M. Reddy est entre elles.

8.11.1987
Amina

June 20, 1988
Mothers are safeguarding Mr. Reddy's body.

20. Juni 1988
Mütter beschützen Herrn Reddys Körper.

20 juin 1988
Les Mères protègent le corps de M. Reddy.

PUBLISHERS' NOTE

The publishers are very grateful to the photographer Philipp Schönborn and the many translators who have worked on this project for their contribution to this volume and for the generosity of spirit in which it was offered.

The quote on page 3 is taken from *The Mother* by Adilakshmi Olati, Mother Meera Publications, 1987. A French edition of this work, *La Lumière de Mère Meera*, was published by L'Or du Temps in 1988. Both volumes are available from Mother Meera, Oberdorf 4A (or Langgasse 4), D-6255 Dornburg-Thalheim, West Germany.